Jennifer

Honouring Heart

May you touch dragonflies and stars,

dance with fairies and talk to the moon.

Unknown

Dwell on the beauty of life.
Watch the stars, and see yourself
running with them.

Marcus Aurelius

With self belief

nothing is impossible

An oyster who was not injured,
will never produce pearls,
because the pearl
is a healed wound.

Anon

In this world I paddle
my own canoe

Thanks, Deb for being
unapologetically you

Deborah Vaimarasi Rasiga
14/8/1959 – 23/9/2021

Give yourself permission

to be your own light

before you shine

on others

Hey, you.

Yes, you.

You really are a beautiful soul.

Have you told yourself that lately?

I can hear your mind speaking to you.

I know you can hear it too.

But are you listening?

Most of us don't say these words to ourselves even though we may say them to others throughout our day. This journal is a reminder to you to spend small moments throughout the day, reflecting on you. Just you and how you might be feeling.

You spend so much time giving to others – your partner, parents, children, neighbour's, strangers, work mates. You smile as you listen and bring happiness and kindness into their worlds.

But what about your world?

When was the last time you checked in and listened to you?

When was the last time you reflected on who you are and your needs?

Expressing gratitude and reflecting on who you are, setting daily intentions, is not being selfish. It's keeping your cup full. It's daily self-care that educates the heart, your heart, for total alignment – mind, body and soul.

transform

illuminate

adapt

grow

change

wisdom

clarity

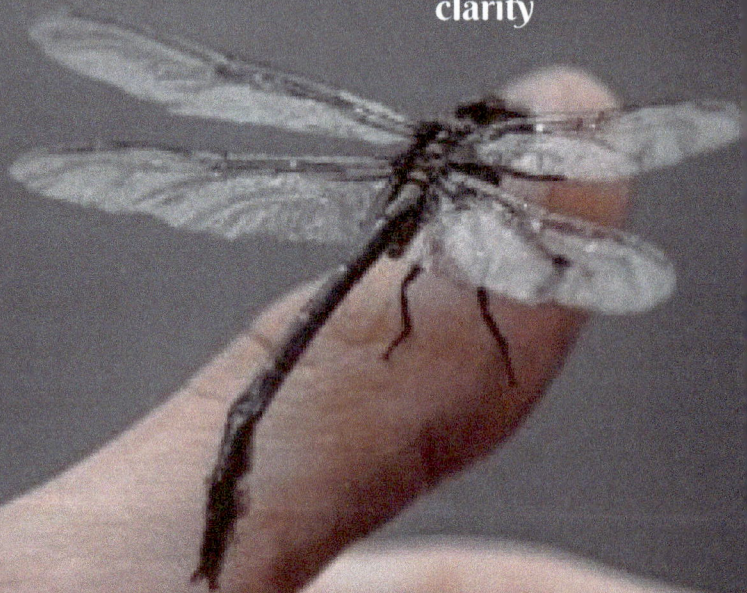

This journal provides a safe space for you to record and reflect on your daily habits and the amount of self care you give yourself over 21 days. Most of all, it's in tick and flick form, purposefully built this way so it can be done when having a cup of tea, and also, when viewed, gives an overall evaluation in one quick glance.

Take these moments just for you.

Reflect on your day.

Can you see patterns emerging?

Our days feed our souls.

How is yours feeling right now?

Should you be a little kinder to yourself?

Is your mind and your soul

in total alignment

with your heart?

Love you

All of you

For all time.

Love your mistakes.

Love your successes.

Love your weaknesses.

Love your strengths.

Surround yourself

with rays of sunshine

That lift, not deplete.

Love your shadows.

Love your happiness.

Love you

All of you

For all time.

Talk to yourself

like you would

to someone

you love

Brené Brown

Know Yourself

The following pages ask you to
explore the true nature of your
character and to consider what you
do and don't like emotionally,
mentally, physically.

You will find clarity, honing values
and goals for you – making time and
space to support and nurture
yourself from within.

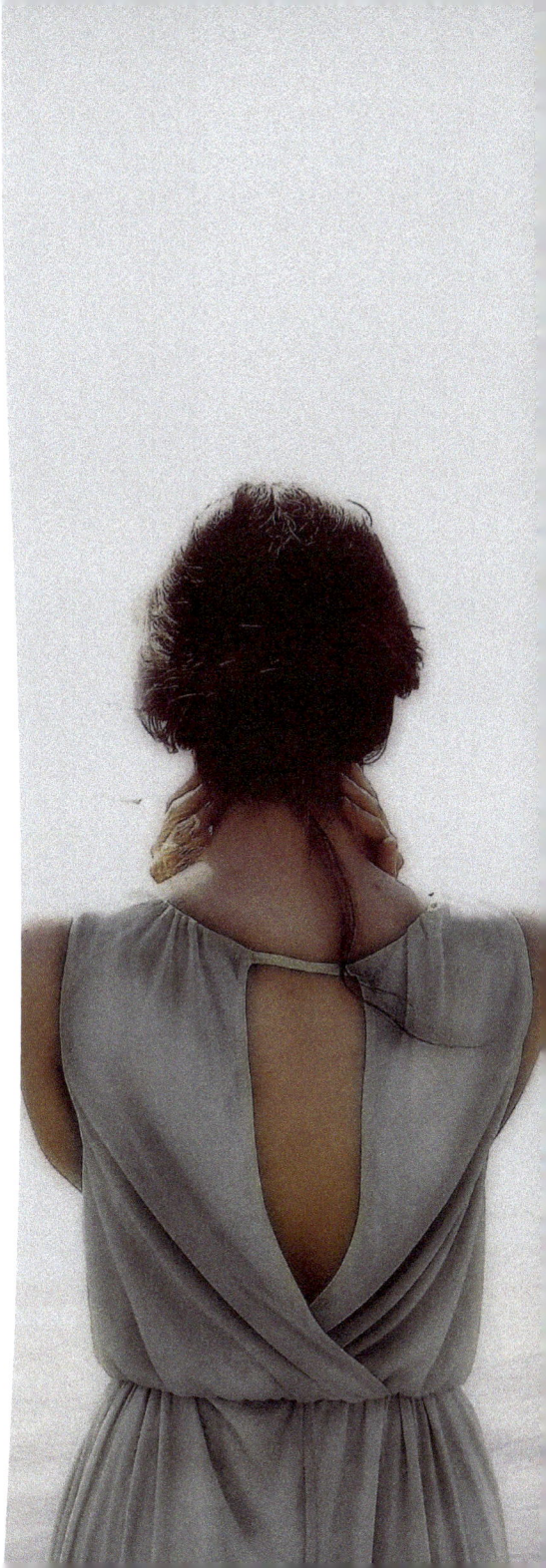

What does self care look like to you?

I want you to take a moment to have a look at yourself and think about what self-care means to you.

Using the exercises on the following pages, explore what self care means specifically for you. Maybe it's taking that walk, drinking water, listening to music. Whatever it is, take the time to reflect on this and write it down.

Are you fully engaged with your self care? Do you nurture it? Is the synergy there?

On the following pages, get to know yourself. Be honest about how much self care you really give yourself and what really matters to you.

Are you following the crowd, or are you in sync with your inner being? In other words –

Are
you
Honouring
Your
Heart?

Think about who are you? Do you really know you well enough to care properly for yourself?

What do you think of you?

Write down 5 words that you feel describe you. Don't overthink it. Write down what comes immediately to mind. Be honest. Don't write down what you think others may think of you.

You need to know what YOU think of YOU.

1. _____
_____

2. _____
_____

3. _____
_____

4. _____
_____

5. _____
_____

Using these five words, write down what each of them
mean to you. Once again, don't overthink it.
What is your gut telling you?

1. _____
   _____
   _____
   _____
   _____
   _____

2. _____
   _____
   _____
   _____
   _____

3. _____
   _____
   _____
   _____
   _____
   _____

4. _____
_____
_____
_____
_____
_____

5. _____
_____
_____
_____
_____
_____

Fear is a reaction.

Courage is a decision.

Sir Winston Churchill

Use the following pages to write down your thoughts, ideas, beliefs, values about what you know about self care and be honest with yourself about how much you practice it. Honesty is key.

From little things big things grow

If only I was...

It's important to accept and love the person you are. Go back to the five words you came up with that you think describe you. Note below any character traits you see. Are you feeling good about you or is there space for growth? What is it that you dislike about yourself and why? Write down your thoughts on how you may be able to change these beliefs about yourself that will enable positive thinking.

_____

_____

_____

_____

_____

_____

_____

_____

_____

_____

_____

_____

_____

_____

_____

_____

Knowledge speaks

Wisdom listens

Anon

Your
time
is
now

The following pages
provide you space for 21
days to find out how well
you are doing.

They are a daily check-ins
with yourself to see how
you are going.

The first page sets your daily intention

for the beginning

of each day.

The second page

is a daily reflection

to be filled out

at the end of the day.

Let's begin...

It is my intention today to:

_____

_____

How did I feel when I first woke today? Sluggish, tired, negative, grumpy, happy, positive.

_____

_____

How did I sleep? How many hours did I sleep for?

_____

_____

Did I dream? Nightmare? Neither?

_____

_____

Breakfast	
Lunch	
Dinner	
In-between	
drinks	

Will I do any exercise, or will I be a potato couch?

_____

What other activities will I do? Cook, clean, play with my animals, be social, create, meditate, give to others, me time, learn...

_____

Daily Reflection

Today I physically feel?

__ rested   __stressed   __sluggish

__ strong   __relaxed   __ weak

__energized   __tired   __positive

What did I do for others today?

_____

_____

What did I do for me today?

_____

_____

How do I feel emotionally?

_____

_____

Is my cup half full or half empty?

_____

_____

My affirmation for tomorrow

_____

_____

_____

_____

_____

It is my intention today to:

_____

_____

How did I feel when I first woke today? Sluggish, tired, negative, grumpy, happy, positive.

_____

_____

How did I sleep? How many hours did I sleep for?

_____

_____

Did I dream? Nightmare? Neither?

_____

_____

Breakfast	
Lunch	
Dinner	
In-between	
drinks	

Will I do any exercise, or will I be a potato couch?

_____

What other activities will I do? Cook, clean, play with my animals, be social, create, meditate, give to others, me time, learn...

_____

Daily Reflection

Today I physically feel?

__ rested   __stressed   __sluggish

__ strong   __relaxed   __ weak

__energized   __tired   __positive

What did I do for others today?

_____

_____

What did I do for me today?

_____

_____

How do I feel emotionally?

_____

_____

Is my cup half full or half empty?

_____

_____

My affirmation for tomorrow

_____

_____

_____

_____

_____

It is my intention today to:

_____

_____

How did I feel when I first woke today? Sluggish, tired, negative, grumpy, happy, positive.

_____

_____

How did I sleep? How many hours did I sleep for?

_____

_____

Did I dream? Nightmare? Neither?

_____

_____

Breakfast	
Lunch	
Dinner	
In-between	
drinks	

Will I do any exercise, or will I be a potato couch?

_____

What other activities will I do? Cook, clean, play with my animals, be social, create, meditate, give to others, me time, learn...

_____

Daily Reflection

Today I physically feel?

__ rested	__stressed	__sluggish
__ strong	__relaxed	__ weak
__energized	__tired	__positive

What did I do for others today?

_____

_____

What did I do for me today?

_____

_____

How do I feel emotionally?

_____

_____

Is my cup half full or half empty?

_____

_____

My affirmation for tomorrow

_____

_____

_____

_____

_____

It is my intention today to:

_____

_____

How did I feel when I first woke today? Sluggish, tired, negative, grumpy, happy, positive.

_____

_____

How did I sleep? How many hours did I sleep for?

_____

_____

Did I dream? Nightmare? Neither?

_____

_____

Breakfast	
Lunch	
Dinner	
In-between	
drinks	

Will I do any exercise, or will I be a potato couch?

_____

What other activities will I do? Cook, clean, play with my animals, be social, create, meditate, give to others, me time, learn...

_____

Daily Reflection

Today I physically feel?

__ rested   __stressed   __sluggish

__ strong   __relaxed   __ weak

__energized   __tired   __positive

What did I do for others today?
_____
_____

What did I do for me today?
_____
_____

How do I feel emotionally?
_____
_____

Is my cup half full or half empty?
_____
_____

My affirmation for tomorrow

_____

_____

_____

_____

_____

It is my intention today to:

_____

_____

How did I feel when I first woke today? Sluggish, tired, negative, grumpy, happy, positive.

_____

_____

How did I sleep? How many hours did I sleep for?

_____

_____

Did I dream? Nightmare? Neither?

_____

_____

Breakfast	
Lunch	
Dinner	
In-between	
drinks	

Will I do any exercise, or will I be a potato couch?

_____

What other activities will I do? Cook, clean, play with my animals, be social, create, meditate, give to others, me time, learn...

_____

Daily Reflection

Today I physically feel?

__ rested   __stressed   __sluggish

__ strong   __relaxed   __ weak

__energized   __tired   __positive

What did I do for others today?

_____

_____

What did I do for me today?

_____

_____

How do I feel emotionally?

_____

_____

Is my cup half full or half empty?

_____

_____

My affirmation for tomorrow

_____

_____

_____

_____

_____

It is my intention today to:

_____

_____

How did I feel when I first woke today? Sluggish, tired, negative, grumpy, happy, positive.

_____

_____

How did I sleep? How many hours did I sleep for?

_____

_____

Did I dream? Nightmare? Neither?

_____

_____

Breakfast	
Lunch	
Dinner	
In-between	
drinks	

Will I do any exercise, or will I be a potato couch?

_____

What other activities will I do? Cook, clean, play with my animals, be social, create, meditate, give to others, me time, learn...

_____

Daily Reflection

Today I physically feel?

__ rested   __stressed   __sluggish

__ strong   __relaxed   __ weak

__energized   __tired   __positive

What did I do for others today?
_____
_____

What did I do for me today?
_____
_____

How do I feel emotionally?
_____
_____

Is my cup half full or half empty?
_____
_____

My affirmation for tomorrow

_____

_____

_____

_____

_____

It is my intention today to:

_____

_____

How did I feel when I first woke today? Sluggish, tired, negative, grumpy,
happy, positive.

_____

_____

How did I sleep? How many hours did I sleep for?

_____

Did I dream? Nightmare? Neither?

_____

What will I eat today?

Breakfast	
Lunch	
Dinner	
In-between	
drinks	

Will I do any exercise, or will I be a potato couch?

_____

What other activities will I do? Cook, clean, play with my animals, be social,
create, meditate, give to others, me time, learn...

_____

Daily Reflection

Today I physically feel?

__ rested   __stressed   __sluggish

__ strong   __relaxed   __ weak

__energized   __tired   __positive

What did I do for others today?

_____

_____

What did I do for me today?

_____

_____

How do I feel emotionally?

_____

_____

Is my cup half full or half empty?

_____

_____

My affirmation for tomorrow

_____

_____

_____

_____

_____

Find the love you seek,
By first finding the love within
yourself.
Learn to rest in that place within
you
that is your true home.

Sri Ravi Shankar

She silently stepped out of the
race she never wanted to be in,
found her own lane
and proceeded
to win

Anon

It is my intention today to:

_____

_____

How did I feel when I first woke today? Sluggish, tired, negative, grumpy, happy, positive.

_____

_____

How did I sleep? How many hours did I sleep for?

_____

_____

Did I dream? Nightmare? Neither?

_____

_____

Breakfast	
Lunch	
Dinner	
In-between	
drinks	

Will I do any exercise, or will I be a potato couch?

_____

What other activities will I do? Cook, clean, play with my animals, be social, create, meditate, give to others, me time, learn...

_____

Daily Reflection

Today I physically feel?

__ rested   __stressed   __sluggish

__ strong   __relaxed   __ weak

__energized   __tired   __positive

What did I do for others today?

_____

_____

What did I do for me today?

_____

_____

How do I feel emotionally?

_____

_____

Is my cup half full or half empty?

_____

_____

My affirmation for tomorrow

_____

_____

_____

_____

_____

It is my intention today to:

_____

_____

How did I feel when I first woke today? Sluggish, tired, negative, grumpy, happy, positive.

_____

_____

How did I sleep? How many hours did I sleep for?

_____

_____

Did I dream? Nightmare? Neither?

_____

_____

Breakfast	
Lunch	
Dinner	
In-between	
drinks	

Will I do any exercise, or will I be a potato couch?

_____

What other activities will I do? Cook, clean, play with my animals, be social, create, meditate, give to others, me time, learn...

_____

Daily Reflection

Today I physically feel?

___ rested   ___stressed   ___sluggish

___ strong   ___relaxed   ___ weak

___energized   ___tired   ___positive

What did I do for others today?

_____

_____

What did I do for me today?

_____

_____

How do I feel emotionally?

_____

_____

Is my cup half full or half empty?

_____

_____

My affirmation for tomorrow

_____

_____

_____

_____

_____

It is my intention today to:

_____

_____

How did I feel when I first woke today? Sluggish, tired, negative, grumpy, happy, positive.

_____

_____

How did I sleep? How many hours did I sleep for?

_____

_____

Did I dream? Nightmare? Neither?

_____

_____

Breakfast

Lunch

Dinner

In-between

drinks

Will I do any exercise, or will I be a potato couch?

_____

What other activities will I do? Cook, clean, play with my animals, be social, create, meditate, give to others, me time, learn...

_____

Daily Reflection

Today I physically feel?

__ rested   __stressed   __sluggish

__ strong   __relaxed   __ weak

__energized   __tired   __positive

What did I do for others today?

_____

_____

What did I do for me today?

_____

_____

How do I feel emotionally?

_____

_____

Is my cup half full or half empty?

_____

_____

My affirmation for tomorrow

_____

_____

_____

_____

_____

Daily Intention   Day 11

It is my intention today to:

_____

_____

How did I feel when I first woke today? Sluggish, tired, negative, grumpy, happy, positive.

_____

_____

How did I sleep? How many hours did I sleep for?

_____

_____

Did I dream? Nightmare? Neither?

_____

_____

Breakfast	
Lunch	
Dinner	
In-between	
drinks	

Will I do any exercise, or will I be a potato couch?

_____

What other activities will I do? Cook, clean, play with my animals, be social, create, meditate, give to others, me time, learn...

_____

Daily Reflection

Today I physically feel?

__ rested   __stressed   __sluggish

__ strong   __relaxed   __ weak

__energized   __tired   __positive

What did I do for others today?

_____

_____

What did I do for me today?

_____

_____

How do I feel emotionally?

_____

_____

Is my cup half full or half empty?

_____

_____

My affirmation for tomorrow

_____

_____

_____

_____

_____

It is my intention today to:

_____

_____

How did I feel when I first woke today? Sluggish, tired, negative, grumpy, happy, positive.

_____

_____

How did I sleep? How many hours did I sleep for?

_____

_____

Did I dream? Nightmare? Neither?

_____

_____

Breakfast	
Lunch	
Dinner	
In-between	
drinks	

Will I do any exercise, or will I be a potato couch?

_____

What other activities will I do? Cook, clean, play with my animals, be social, create, meditate, give to others, me time, learn...

_____

Daily Reflection

Today I physically feel?

__ rested   __stressed   __sluggish

__ strong   __relaxed   __ weak

__energized   __tired   __positive

What did I do for others today?
_____
_____

What did I do for me today?
_____
_____

How do I feel emotionally?
_____
_____

Is my cup half full or half empty?
_____
_____

My affirmation for tomorrow

_____

_____

_____

_____

_____

It is my intention today to:

_____

_____

How did I feel when I first woke today? Sluggish, tired, negative, grumpy, happy, positive.

_____

_____

How did I sleep? How many hours did I sleep for?

_____

_____

Did I dream? Nightmare? Neither?

_____

_____

Breakfast	
Lunch	
Dinner	
In-between	
drinks	

Will I do any exercise, or will I be a potato couch?

_____

What other activities will I do? Cook, clean, play with my animals, be social, create, meditate, give to others, me time, learn...

_____

Daily Reflection

Today I physically feel?

__ rested   __stressed   __sluggish

__ strong   __relaxed   __ weak

__energized   __tired   __positive

What did I do for others today?

_____

_____

What did I do for me today?

_____

_____

How do I feel emotionally?

_____

_____

Is my cup half full or half empty?

_____

_____

My affirmation for tomorrow

_____

_____

_____

_____

_____

It is my intention today to:

_____

_____

How did I feel when I first woke today? Sluggish, tired, negative, grumpy, happy, positive.

_____

_____

How did I sleep? How many hours did I sleep for?

_____

_____

Did I dream? Nightmare? Neither?

_____

_____

Breakfast	
Lunch	
Dinner	
In-between	
drinks	

Will I do any exercise, or will I be a potato couch?

_____

What other activities will I do? Cook, clean, play with my animals, be social, create, meditate, give to others, me time, learn...

_____

Daily Reflection

Today I physically feel?

__ rested   __stressed   __sluggish

__ strong   __relaxed   __ weak

__energized   __tired   __positive

What did I do for others today?

_____

_____

What did I do for me today?

_____

_____

How do I feel emotionally?

_____

_____

Is my cup half full or half empty?

_____

_____

My affirmation for tomorrow

_____

_____

_____

_____

_____

To be beautiful means to be yourself.
You don't need to be accepted by
others. You need to accept yourself.
Thich Nhat Hanh

Beauty begins the moment you

decide to be yourself

Coco Chanel

It is my intention today to:

_____

_____

How did I feel when I first woke today? Sluggish, tired, negative, grumpy, happy, positive.

_____

_____

How did I sleep? How many hours did I sleep for?

_____

_____

Did I dream? Nightmare? Neither?

_____

_____

Breakfast

Lunch

Dinner

In-between

drinks

Will I do any exercise, or will I be a potato couch?

_____

What other activities will I do? Cook, clean, play with my animals, be social, create, meditate, give to others, me time, learn...

_____

Daily Reflection

Today I physically feel?

__ rested   __stressed   __sluggish

__ strong   __relaxed   __ weak

__energized   __tired   __positive

What did I do for others today?

_____

_____

What did I do for me today?

_____

_____

How do I feel emotionally?

_____

_____

Is my cup half full or half empty?

_____

_____

My affirmation for tomorrow

_____

_____

_____

_____

_____

It is my intention today to:

_____

_____

How did I feel when I first woke today? Sluggish, tired, negative, grumpy, happy, positive.

_____

_____

How did I sleep? How many hours did I sleep for?

_____

_____

Did I dream? Nightmare? Neither?

_____

_____

Breakfast	
Lunch	
Dinner	
In-between	
drinks	

Will I do any exercise, or will I be a potato couch?

_____

What other activities will I do? Cook, clean, play with my animals, be social, create, meditate, give to others, me time, learn...

_____

Daily Reflection

Today I physically feel?

__ rested   __stressed   __sluggish

__ strong   __relaxed   __ weak

__energized   __tired   __positive

What did I do for others today?

_____

_____

What did I do for me today?

_____

_____

How do I feel emotionally?

_____

_____

Is my cup half full or half empty?

_____

_____

My affirmation for tomorrow

_____

_____

_____

_____

_____

Daily Intention   Day 17

It is my intention today to:

_____

_____

How did I feel when I first woke today? Sluggish, tired, negative, grumpy, happy, positive.

_____

_____

How did I sleep? How many hours did I sleep for?

_____

_____

Did I dream? Nightmare? Neither?

_____

_____

Breakfast	
Lunch	
Dinner	
In-between	
drinks	

Will I do any exercise, or will I be a potato couch?

_____

What other activities will I do? Cook, clean, play with my animals, be social, create, meditate, give to others, me time, learn...

_____

Daily Reflection

Today I physically feel?

__ rested   __stressed   __sluggish

__ strong   __relaxed   __ weak

__energized   __tired   __positive

What did I do for others today?

_____

_____

What did I do for me today?

_____

_____

How do I feel emotionally?

_____

_____

Is my cup half full or half empty?

_____

_____

My affirmation for tomorrow

_____

_____

_____

_____

_____

It is my intention today to:

_____

_____

How did I feel when I first woke today? Sluggish, tired, negative, grumpy, happy, positive.

_____

_____

How did I sleep? How many hours did I sleep for?

_____

_____

Did I dream? Nightmare? Neither?

_____

_____

Breakfast	
Lunch	
Dinner	
In-between	
drinks	

Will I do any exercise, or will I be a potato couch?

_____

What other activities will I do? Cook, clean, play with my animals, be social, create, meditate, give to others, me time, learn…

_____

Daily Reflection

Today I physically feel?

__ rested   __stressed   __sluggish

__ strong   __relaxed   __ weak

__energized   __tired   __positive

What did I do for others today?

_____

_____

What did I do for me today?

_____

_____

How do I feel emotionally?

_____

_____

Is my cup half full or half empty?

_____

_____

My affirmation for tomorrow

_____

_____

_____

_____

_____

It is my intention today to:

_____

_____

How did I feel when I first woke today? Sluggish, tired, negative, grumpy, happy, positive.

_____

_____

How did I sleep? How many hours did I sleep for?

_____

_____

Did I dream? Nightmare? Neither?

_____

_____

Breakfast

Lunch

Dinner

In-between

drinks

Will I do any exercise, or will I be a potato couch?

_____

What other activities will I do? Cook, clean, play with my animals, be social, create, meditate, give to others, me time, learn...

_____

Daily Reflection

Today I physically feel?

__ rested   __stressed   __sluggish

__ strong   __relaxed   __ weak

__energized   __tired   __positive

What did I do for others today?

_____

_____

What did I do for me today?

_____

_____

How do I feel emotionally?

_____

_____

Is my cup half full or half empty?

_____

_____

My affirmation for tomorrow

_____

_____

_____

_____

_____

Daily Intention   Day 20

It is my intention today to:

_____

_____

How did I feel when I first woke today? Sluggish, tired, negative, grumpy, happy, positive.

_____

_____

How did I sleep? How many hours did I sleep for?

_____

_____

Did I dream? Nightmare? Neither?

_____

_____

Breakfast	
Lunch	
Dinner	
In-between	
drinks	

Will I do any exercise, or will I be a potato couch?

_____

What other activities will I do? Cook, clean, play with my animals, be social, create, meditate, give to others, me time, learn...

_____

Daily Reflection

Today I physically feel?

___ rested   ___stressed   ___sluggish

___ strong   ___relaxed   ___ weak

___energized   ___tired   ___positive

What did I do for others today?

_____

_____

What did I do for me today?

_____

_____

How do I feel emotionally?

_____

_____

Is my cup half full or half empty?

_____

_____

My affirmation for tomorrow

_____

_____

_____

_____

_____

It is my intention today to:

_____

_____

How did I feel when I first woke today? Sluggish, tired, negative, grumpy, happy, positive.

_____

_____

How did I sleep? How many hours did I sleep for?

_____

_____

Did I dream? Nightmare? Neither?

_____

_____

Breakfast	
Lunch	
Dinner	
In-between	
drinks	

Will I do any exercise, or will I be a potato couch?

_____

What other activities will I do? Cook, clean, play with my animals, be social, create, meditate, give to others, me time, learn...

_____

Daily Reflection

Today I physically feel?

__ rested   __stressed   __sluggish

__ strong   __relaxed   __ weak

__energized   __tired   __positive

What did I do for others today?

_____

_____

What did I do for me today?

_____

_____

How do I feel emotionally?

_____

_____

Is my cup half full or half empty?

_____

_____

My affirmation for tomorrow

_____

_____

_____

_____

_____

Growth begins when
we start to accept
our own weakness

Jean Vanier

Now you have been setting intentions and doing daily reflections for 21 days,

how are you feeling emotionally and physically?

Can you see any patterns emerging?

I am proud of you for coming this far.

Are YOU proud of YOU?

Write down your immediate thoughts. Don't overthink it.

_____

_____

_____

_____

_____

_____

_____

_____

_____

_____

_____

_____

_____

_____

Thinking about the patterns you have reflected on,

Consider what it is you are going to do to

Honour your Heart.

What are your self care
commitments and
what are you going to let go of?

I commit to doing more of:

_____

_____

_____

_____

_____

_____

_____

_____

_____

_____

_____

_____

_____

_____

I commit to doing less of:

_____

_____

_____

_____

_____

_____

_____

_____

_____

_____

_____

_____

_____

_____

_____

In your commitment to yourself,

allow space for nurturing your spiritual side.

On the opposite page, I've listed what I personally do for me.

Make a list of what you can do for you.

Think about all that interests you and who,

or what, can support you on your journey.

How can learning about this support you back to being you?

What is it that you love that will nurture your soul

and help your energy to flow again?

I want to learn more about:

_____

_____

_____

_____

_____

_____

_____

_____

_____

_____

_____

_____

_____

_____

crystals

tarot

the elements

plants

moon cycles

meditation

mindfulness

dragonflies

visualization

herbs

It's important that you do learn to honour your spiritual side –
whatever that may be for you.

It's our knowing, that gut feeling,

the sixth sense that we all need to honour.

Honouring our spiritual side is surrendering to who we really are

and accepting what is and what will be.

It allows us grace and to flow in life with gratitude.

Explore what you want to learn about. Continuously.

Research and practice it. The more you practice

what you learn the more awareness you will

have. Meditate and become mindful,

not mind full.

Become you

Know you

Honour

Heart

This journal has come to an end but for you

its just the beginning.

Reflect on your notes, summarise

what you have learned.

Set priorities for yourself and make them

very clear not only to yourself, but to those

around you.

What are you going to leave behind?

Let go of?

Get rid of all negative patterns – emotionally and

physically that occur in your life.

What are you going to do more of?

For you and only you?

Create new patterns for you.

What have you committed to?

Begin today. Not tomorrow. Not next week.

Not next month.

Your future to

Honouring Your Heart

begins

now.

Never bend your head.
Always hold it high.
Look the world straight
in the face.

Helen Keller

Celebrate your successes
And stand strong...
The eagle soars,
While the small birds
Take cover.

Napolean Hill

About the Author

Jennifer is a multi-published author of children's picture books, romance, and self-help books and books on successful authorship.

She also is the founder of Daisy Lane Publishing, an award-winning publishing house with national and international award-winning authors. She loves bringing stories to life in all their different forms and sharing them with the world. Jennifer also loves teaching about the writing and publishing process through her coaching and mentoring programs.

When she doesn't have her head in a book either writing one or reading it, with a coffee in hand and cat on knee, you'll find her playing on the beach with her bestie furballs.

A catalogue record for this work is available from the National Library of Australia

NATIONAL LIBRARY OF AUSTRALIA

National library of Australia Catalogue-In-Publication data:

Honouring Heart/Jennifer Sharp

Book Cover Art © 2022 https://www.canva.com
Internal Images © 2022 https://www.canva.com

ISBN: (SC) 9780648904557

CPSIA information can be obtained
at www.ICGtesting.com
Printed in the USA
LVHW071155280222
712191LV00010B/110